the sure
song
of
here

*the writer's cut*

anna cassedy o'neill

**copyright © 2025 by anna cassedy o'neill**

all rights reserved. this book or parts thereof may not be produced in any form without permission.

for permission requests, speaking and writing inquiries please contact:
connect@cassoneill.com
www.cassoneill.com
thisonemagiclife.substack.com
instagram: @cassedyoneill

*cover photo of author taken in the mountains of california by:* suki smith *praise for the sure song of here from readers*

"if you have ever thought that there is more for you in this world than what's written inside the box, this collection is for you. cassedy captures the spirit of belonging in your own skin, and then taking flight from there."

"cassedy brings pisces in full force here, delivering a precious soul gem and a potent piece of heart truth for all to see in plain sight. she is fierce, melodic, and measured in her writer's voice while also claiming dimensions of freedom previously unknown or unseen."

"the sure song of here is a potent and powerful collection of poems that mirror back to you so many parts of yourself you didn't even know existed or needed to be acknowledged. these words will help support and encourage you to bravely take the next steps into the fullest expression of yourself!"

unclench your jaw. relax your shoulders. take a breath from the deepest part of your belly. feel your breath rise up into your chest. hold it there. *feel. feel. feel it all.* slowly exhale. let it go. *let something go.* sit. be. take another deep breath. relax your shoulders even more. open your heart. empty your mind. find yourself here. not in the movement of the world out there, but in the preciousness of your life *right here.* exhale. slowly. feel the bottom of the breath. return.

here you are. here you are. here you are.

the sure song of here *THE WRITER'S CUT* is the version that is the truest from my heart.. it is the bold version, with no cuts from any of the poems and 20 added poems. it is the fullest expression of this book, and one that has been on my heart to release into the world – for her song is powerful, bold, and pure.

may these words land on your heart like raindrops down the window. may your remembrance be kind and soft like the sway of pebbles coming together in the bottom of a river. may your whole world open to what is already here. may you always return to the rhythm of love and find reasons to look up every day and smile at your wild existence. may you thrive. may you dance. may you remember the ripples that you create. *that you matter.* that you are more powerful than the flame in front of your eyes. may this book bring you home.

this book has been birthed from one way tickets. broken hearts. warming hellos. tearful goodbyes. direct messages from mother earth. morning coffee walks. afternoon dance breaks. fresh air. cold showers. sitting on buses and planes and trains. in the stillness of moments in between. as sensations land into words on a page somehow allowing life to make a little more sense. a soul retrieval, of sorts. this book is the pulse of my life. the lens in which i've cracked through. cried through. screamed through. laughed through. learned through. loved through. and lived through. continually being reminded that my hidden wings are safe to fly free in this wild world, and yours are too.

there is a place inside
so still —
that not even a speck of a hurricane
can touch
not even a wave
from the depths
of the oceans
tongue
can quake

there is a place inside
that sleeps
with love and beauty

a place where the
sky illuminates
every part to
have its moment

and yet the pulse
the cadence
the rhythm
is held
in stillness by
**the sure**
**song**

**of here** —

right here
and nowhere to go
no one to be
no one to impress

for the yellow bush
dances in her glory

from within

# the sure songs

to break ............................................. 1
to begin ..........................................55
to build ..................................... 107
to believe ................................. 157
to belong ................................208

# to break

to break

there is a fire
brewing
inside
i can feel it roar
at the space it's
been given to speak
+ be
freely

i can feel the sacredness
to that which it
burns away

there is a purpose
in its every whisper
of truth
as it first arrives
on my heart

breath in
breath out —

here it is
still knocking its
medicinal whisper
holding mirror

## to break

to that which i've tolerated
for too long
energies
people
stories
and their tendrils
poking into my field
no longer — the fire begins to yell
"no longer"
n o l o n g e r
no longer
no longer

i feel it
sacred lines
of boundaries drawn

no more moments
of vultures
gripping their teeth
into my meat

*this vessel is sacred*
*you are sacred*
this fire begins to feel heard

voice finally given to the part

                    to break

inside who finds the treasure
amongst all —

wildfires
clear the path
to that which
no longer
feeds
the flame

## to break

i want you uncontained
on the edge of it all
dripping
in sensation
of hurling yourself
off the cliff
of familiar
into canyons below
clouds above

i want you unfamiliar
to the scent of you
the gaze
you meet in the mirror
the way your hands feel
as you stroke the old leather couch

i want you foreign
to your own concept
and all that you used to reach for

realizing
the forever expansive
breath of you
and the greater *we* at play

i want you barefoot to your own soul

## to break

trusting in the pull of it all
leaving you in blinks
of light
all around
flashes of faraway lands
until this one here lands
as your own

only to leave it all again

i want you naked
raw
exposed to the truth
every cell attuned
to the depth of this life
when you give it all up
to god

## to break

do you see
that hour by hour,
moment by moment,
we are the creators of our
own realities?

do you see
that this is the beginning
of anything you want?

today
this moment
this time
this morning
you have a choice
you have a choice
followed by another choice
followed by another choice

and that's the dance of life

choice by choice
step by step
moment by moment

what will you choose?

## to break

you may ask
and not get answers
you may beg
and your plea may not be heard
people will tell you *can't*
that you *shouldn't*
that it *makes no sense*

your pursuit of your own liberty
will trigger other's fear

don't stop there
at other people's fears
at the small voices trying to
keep you as you are

let your questions remain unanswered
let your pleas remain unheard
let this ignite the spark
that keeps you on your quest for magic

let the thirst of the unknown
satiate your adventures of the known

## to break

do not mistake me for a fool
just because i love
do not mistake me as a show
just because i sing

do not mistake me
as calm waters
when i
am dripping wet
with fire

these teeth
know when to grip
this jaw knows
when to clench
these fists
know when to punch
all in the way
of me
and my vast sky

do not mistake me
for what i am not

               to break

for i am present to
my own medicine
and the golden rage
of this yell

## to break

can we finally let go
and believe the stories
underneath
that hold the torch
for what is true
can we finally let go
and believe in the world
of us
beneath the surface of this life
only touched when we breathe
it all the way in

to break

    the pausing
      the question asking
      the mirror looking
    not glancing
    but looking
    *really looking*
    until all shatters
    all dissolves
      except the pulse
      and beating power
    of truth
    being witnessed
    with your clear eyes

to break

we don't have to carry
the heaviness anymore
it's okay
we can put it down
and find our wings here

## to break

i slip into now
immerse myself so deeply
into the feelings
of this present scene

anything not in service
of here
slips away
floats on
down the river
around its own bend
for its own journey

not for one more moment
will i allow myself to feel like a burden
a second choice
to someone else's present scene

allowing the invisible wall
of separation
cause this togetherness
to fade

not for one more moment
will i take part of this story
that beats no life

                              to break

for the life of us

## to break

did you feel that emotion swell?
in the core of you?
right over your heart

it's the reminder of your aliveness
and all the impermanence
that comes with it

you will never have this moment again
you will never be this exact person
in this exact moment

your eyes will shift
and so will you

so can you feel it?
allow it?

every sensation
mixing and arriving
at the death and rebirth
of it all

this life too glorious

to break

too precious
for us not to allow
those feelings
to stir us into
the hurricane
of everything inside

## to break

the day will come when you can no longer hold onto the boulders of rock around you. when you can no longer hold onto the safety nets of the hearts of those around you. feasting on what's easy. and comfortable. and safe. the day will come when you decide to be scared and do it anyway. to let go. to release the grip. to lean into the madness of your heart pulling you down the river. down the flow of life. and when this day comes, let it come. do not resist its treasure. do not resist its essence. when this day comes, celebrate it as your birthday. the day when you no longer decided to carry the story of others as your own. the day you decided to take your own life into your heart. into your hands. into your eyes. the day you decided to make it about you. and not them. let it rinse you clean. let it rip you open. into your heart that bleeds and beats for truth and nothing else. for integrity and nothing else. for alignment and nothing else. then, and only then, will you know what living is all about.

## to break

i see the pattern
the one little tricky
opening
for separation
that causes a landslide
an avalanche
of disconnection
separation
and ripping apart of oneness

it starts as inches
centimeters
tiny tiny tiny
openings
for the traces of stickiness
of the mind
to attach to
like watching dominos fall
and landing us separate
on an island
confused about it all

to break

what do you do when you are surrounded by the voices of those who can't feel what you feel? those who don't speak the language of the subtleties like you do? what do you do then? do you allow the lens of disconnect to fill the connects? all of the places that were once whole? do you fill the blinks of time with knowing that you are exactly where you're meant to be? how can you practice the lens of love even in the spaces where fear wants to close in on you?

to break

it's okay
   to not be okay

## to break

i think it can be too easy to not believe in ourselves. and place the blame on external everything's. it can be too easy to give in to the illusionary land mines all around causing us for however long, to not believe. it can be too easy to forget the breath of something larger. to let ourselves be caught. guided. held. loved. to let go of the reins to something that belongs to our old life. our old ways.

do we hold on, just to learn how to let go?
do we push ourselves to our edges just to see if we will jump?

funny how the answers are right here. funny how everything we want is, too. time collapsing. facades falling. seeing the subconscious beliefs so obviously in front. like pulling out the deepest weeds inside. here to set it all free.

## to break

give in
to what is given

everything breaking down
around you
finding your place
amongst chaos
alive by the mind

nothing is wrong here
no wrong turns
it simply all is

you are seeing
with the most sober eyes

and in the seeing
comes the clearing

## to break

eyes flutter open
to that which
they cannot hide from
anymore
eyelids blink open
to that which they
cannot be blind to anymore

what they don't tell you
is that a death
is an awakening
certain parts of you
finally open
to the truth
that other parts of you
must be transmuted
and go to sleep forever

where do dogs go when they die?
heaven they say

let your dissolved parts
go be free
to go be heaven
to play
in rainbows

to break

with rivers
and creeks
and streams
and giddiness
and laughter
and unbridled joy
the kind you can taste from afar
as you walk on
bravely and boldly
without

to break



our closing
created
my opening

to break

how much tenderness do you need dear heart? in order for you to know it's safe for you to soften in moments when the world screams for you harden? for you to know that permission must be granted in order for you to close the gates of heavens around your beautiful pulse? how much kindness and forgiveness can you lend me in these moments when all i want to do is hurl over and bury my head into a pillow until i awaken into a world where my baby is in my arms. and the world is moving a little slower. with a little bit more love for all of the different colors of humanity. for all of the different brushstrokes of brilliance.

## to break

i hold on to her,
like somehow she is lost
like somehow i am not me
anymore
and i'm trying to get back to her
is it just the looks
or the feeling of freedom
and expression she had?
what got caked on in layers
of life i didn't say no to?
and why do i keep looking
back at her?
what key is she still holding
of my presence?
did i leave part of my
soul in california?
and when i return will i
find once again
the feeling i can only
remember in photos?
oh how i crave
to be that woman
again

to break

this is a conversation
with surrender
and surrender
begs to be met
with trust
and trust
can only be met
in this present moment
dropping my knees
to mother earth and feeling it all

## to break

how do we get out of this story
built and marked
by these walls
habits formed by environment
how do we burn down the walls
that cause purpose to this flame?

for the hearts
of many
to come together as one

for the aching to be verbalized
instead of gulped down

for the words to be spoken
instead of yelled

for laughter to be fed
instead of judgement

for more of what floats us and not sinks us

so that we don't have to escape or run and jump
and hide
so that nothing takes power over the power of the
love in this house

## to break

love wants to be king here
love wants to be here
love wants to live here
thrive here

be felt here

can we take a pause
and shift the wind in these sails?

our ship has already sunk, the longer
we stay here, the more irrevocable
damage is done
like two bullet holes in the basin
destined
for the bottom of the ocean
destined to rust
for scuba divers to one day piece together
the missing pieces of why we couldn't float
or sail any longer

let's not play to the beat of this tune
let's not allow this to be the backbone
of what we accept as this moment
*no longer*

to break

too much at stake for too long

we are all guilty here

come
place your fingers on my heart
place your other hand on yours
we are family
we beat for the same
we beat for the same
we beat for the same

to break


i get to know
what's mine
and let the rest
burn away

## to break

the tears
reveal the bigness

the heart breaking
reveals the opening

you're going to miss it
this place
this moment
these people
this dog
this room
this everything —
you're going to miss it
but missing it
was never meant to stop you
from living it

missing it
was meant to
shine the light
and bring it
alive for you
as you fade
into another color
of this life

to break

and so
off we go
into the distance
into the limitless potential
of the guidance
from our heart whispers
off we go
with open hearts
hurling into the unknown
crying
feeling
allowing
it all to be
happening
and merging
and existing
in this moment

off we go
into the heart
of the unknown
deeply grounded
in our own

to break

the missing comes in waves
sets of seven
nature's style
*ride it*
i think
just ride the wave
become one with it
let it change you
re-shape you
spit you out anew
we've been given every
surfboard needed
to handle all things
that come our way
these are all part of our ocean
if only we stopped fighting
*life* itself
and just trusted the
power of the ocean
at hand

to break

and in the end,
we say goodbye
to the greatest love
we've ever known
the greatest love
that was never ours
to keep
in the first place

to break

isn't this the wildest part of life? what we *leave behind?* even though it is all footprints on our hearts? traces and lines marked forever. but somehow the concept of forever feels so intangible when it's invisible. seasons change. people come. people go. so do we.

to break


humbled by the way god
slams you back into the passenger seat

## to break

the residue of you
fills blank spaces
with question marks

oxygen pressed
into the tea kettle
bound for an explosion

swirls of familiar scents
and touches
deliver themselves
in the costume
of nostalgia

do i answer the door?
do i allow the lungs of yesterday
to breathe into today?

you appear
like the pioneer
that you were —
absorbing punches
of that which caused direction
to your compass
your true north
ancient wisdom

## to break

buried beneath the story
of what was planted
in the garden of others

blood dripped into honey
until we couldn't be anymore

tied too tight
woven too close
no breath here

bring out the applause
for i set sail
to the scent of you

to break

remembering
that everything
comes alive
in the goodbyes

## to break

when you miss them,
*miss them fully*
feel the feeling all the
way in
let the thread touch the
most tender part inside
let it speak
until you feel
the sacredness of this life
the pieces of impermanence
that allow you to live
a little more into your
*nows*

## to break

sometimes it's going to hurt
like shards of rock
cutting directly into
the wound
the place
where it came

sometimes it's going to hurt
and you're not going to know why
it just simply will
and when it does
let it

let it all
crumble around you

the only grip
you were meant to grasp
was the grip
of trust
and surrender
deeper in your bones
than you know

to break

may you find grace
in your fall

to break

and just like that
you're in
and out
you come
and go

to break

nostalgic
for the moments
when you touched
me in those
ways

and we talked
the way
we did
with
our fingertips

the way our tongues
found the story of
why we came to be
and our feet
found the door
of goodbye

to break

new parts of you
hugged and healed

some parts of you
released and returned

forever changed
from being entangled
in places
we just came from

trips are passport stamps
into remembering

## to break

i drove to the edge of it all
put the mirror down
and stared into my eyes

i saw her fierceness
and her broken heart
i saw her openness
and trust
i saw her broken legs
her frustration
and i saw her clarity
her love
her connection

i saw deep
into the spaces
that she only shows
if you stay

i drove to the edge of it all
put the visor mirror down
and i remembered
i remembered that
it is all happening
right here
right here

to break

*right here*

this gaze
these eyes
the thoughts
that land
into the sensation
of truth
and the ones that
roll off like the beads
of sweat
carrying with it
every weight
every story
no longer pulsing
life into this vessel

every sensation
that feels borrowed
and the revolution
inside that deeply belongs

all truths
merging
into one story

i get to decide

## to break

which one
i am dancing with
right now
in this moment

i get to choose
i get to decide

i drove to the edge of it all
and i screamed
released
that which doesn't serve
released
those who don't belong

for these eyes
this story
must keep beating
for the mission
greater than what meets these eyes

for these eyes are the mirror
into so much more
than ever
could be known

all must be lived

to break

right here
in this moment

we came here to feel
*she remembered*
we came here to feel it all

to break

every single step
of this wild path
unraveling
all of what isn't true
so the beat
the pulse
the cadence
of truth
can sing it's sure song
to us all

dimples speak
the loudest truth

you and me
*we*
you and me
*we*

we are free
we are free
we are free

to break

forgive yourself for everything

# to begin

## to begin

i am here,
here i am,
how did i get so far away?
and where did the time go?
and how did i forget?
and what was i looking for anyway?
here i am, it is me
and i am free
free from all of the weight
or the time
free from the stories i
no longer hold as mine
free from what it is
they say we are
supposed to do and be
free to bask in
the delight of what's here
and how i can just go
there whenever i want
whenever i choose
to remember the power
of closing our eyes
and letting the light
tickle our eyelids

## to begin

the heart speaks
in surrender
blinks
of time between light
flashes
blinks of time
between
movement

that moment
when you've dropped into
the space between

expand
contract
badum
badum
badum

it beats for you
the bigness of your life
the bigness of your flight

trapped
in the mind
swirling in stories

## to begin

no longer
meant for you

stopped
at
how simple it all can be

to begin

grabbing a pen,
lighting a candle,
and declaring the moment
as the temple –
the place we enter,
and everything else withers away

to begin

call it what you want
but i call this a return to love
a return to connection
to all living and breathing things
one singular grace
one singular stroke of beauty
one whisper of truth at a time

## to begin

what if we start over?
plant this day
as blank canvas
color me beautiful

## to begin

let the depth of your breath expand
drink in the
tie dye sky

sink into the stillness —
that which guards
your heart

big gulps
of this new life
as you prepare
for what's prepared
for you —

a master mistaken
as an apprentice

if you only knew
how free you always were

empty
empty
empty
the shallow licks
of resistance

to begin

drink
drink
drink
from the pulse
that unclips
your wings —
when you allow it all to be
*right here*
with you

when you allow
it all to
rest —
bury your
heart here
for you are
home with
the red earth

to begin

self love is a
quiet revolution of yes
found in the listening

## to begin

we get stuck
different day
same color
same experience
day after day
*after day*
we shop at the same
grocery stores
drive the same roads
have the same types of
conversations at the
same dinner tables
and then you get
taken to the sea
one tiny new little adventure
and you feel your body open
and feel your head tilt
toward a new way
you remember what it's like
for your senses to come online
for your life to feel like an
adventure once again

to begin

you honor death
by experiencing life

## to begin

reach out your hand
touch mine
grab mine
as we grasp onto us
and the remedy
of that which is to be

## to begin

she slips into the same
white rain boots
headed for a familiar place
but this time
the woman
is different

this flight looks like same
yet this feeling is new

this woman is new

last time she wore these shoes
she was more a young woman
blooming into a woman
en route from maiden
to mother

wearing more
than she needed
to belong

giving her power away
without giving herself
a chance

## to begin

tears bring her home
releasing
the hold

a remodel
*of sorts*

she slips on these white boots

realizing home was never
a place out there
it was a season in here
that wanted to hold her
forever
in its embrace

to begin

who are you *being*
when you are *feeling?*

## to begin

i hope you believe
in beautiful endings
with messy middles
and clear beginnings

*i gently declare this the beginning*

## to begin

maybe we begin here
letting these palms
touch this body

saying i'm sorry
thank you
i love you
please forgive me

for every missed
skipped beat

maybe we start here
cradling our own hold
becoming mother
to self
waving the flag of light

asking what we need
in order to
move forward
begin forward
right here
with this lonely
empty
perfectly
open

## to begin

doorway

when all quiets down
except the whispers
of connection
to this hammock
of time
always held by
the internal pillars
of trust
and truth
unmovable
by that which spins
around it

## to begin

perhaps if we bang our head enough times into a wall, we remember that, this too, is our choosing. this perpetual living with an exploded mind trying to figure it all out. getting stuck by letting the spotlight focus on the sticky flammable parts, not the parts of lightness and air all around that bring us home. perhaps these moments, too, are as important to our humanity as the ones that follow. and the key is of remembrance. remembering the power that we hold. that which we speak from our tongues becomes liquefied into reality before we know it. that which we move with becomes felt and drank up by all those around us. silence only causes daggers to what is felt in the knowing. no escaping this one here. just more feeling. and bashing. until you look in the mirror and catch a tiny corner of the breath. and it all lands home again.

## to begin

strike a match near this body
and the whole city
will engulf in flames

take another stab
at truth
and this whole world
will lift
into flight

speak another lick
of your small self
and you will see
the primal
come out
like a lioness
protective over her cubs

it is life or death
and truth
is life
and anything
that touches this
will turn to ashes

## to begin

one more drop
and we will explode

let it all die
that which is meant to die

and what is meant to grow
let it grow
let it grow
let it grow

## to begin

what happens when the fire burns so hot
you can't help but taste the truth
amongst its ashes

what happens when your backbone
sinks back into place
each part
locking into its home
reminding you of your power
of choice
your holding
of self

what story wants to be written
from this place?
you
with your backbone
you
with the sacred fire
burning
bringing heat
to the places
that moments ago
we're ice
you
with the sacred fire burning

## to begin

reminding you
all that stands around you
is a mystery
you are the pillar
you are the golden one
you've been waiting for all along

when the curtains pull back
when the fog clears from the glasses
and you are present to
that which you didn't want to see

what happens then?

do you close your eyes
and hold your breath?
do you let the prowess of the wind
carry the flame
of the fire
until
all that's meant to be ashed
becomes ash?
until you find the phoenix
inside to rise again?

how quickly pages burn
how quickly chapters end

## to begin

how quickly stories get their closing
right when you thought they were opening

how easily we determine
the grit
of what parts play a role
in it all

how easily we grab on
to the boulders of rock around us
only to arrive back home
into the trust fall
free fall
of it all
as we land
into the pulse
of that which spits truth for us
and nothing else

to begin

open the doors
everything
wants to be seen

to begin

the breathless
constriction
to the full belly
release

*forget to remember*
*contract to expand*

to begin

you must
let the whole
land in the fullness
of the mis-fused
parts
until the licks
turn the wheel
to the diamond
created
from pressure

pressure ignites
what is meant
to be touched
into form

to begin

we don't know
the nature
of the mystery
just the feeling
pulling us there

to begin

rip off the clothes
that fit too tight
burn the stories
that suffocate
your breath
let the rust
of your creaky bones
rise like the dust
taken from the ashes

to begin

new glances
new chances
bring deliverance
to the next
taste of you

## to begin

there is settlement
and power here
and also
the feeling of dizziness
from the lack
of to dos

so we switch to
*to bes*
and let the tides
of it all
take us
into the winds
of a gentle pace
back home

to begin

keep your sights
one step beyond
the invisible line
that tries to stop you
block you
halt you
from all
that is already
yours
ours
for the tending
the impermanence
of it all
every single thing being a visitor
every feeling
every identity of self
every clothing item
every home
innately temporary
to unlock
the permanent
part
of
your
depth

to begin

*the key*

do not ever settle
for anything in this life
let your mind and heart
be completely and utterly
moved
by the magic that is your life

often
we're afraid to leave what we have
and who we're with
and where we are
because we afraid
*it can't get any better than this*
we think
*a story*

*no one will know me
or love me like this
no place will ever accept me like this
a story*

and we crucify our own lives
by believing these loops

*none of that is true*

## to begin

if you live a life
devoted to the raw truth
and nothing else
you will be mind blown
heart blown
world blown
at how truly good and
beautiful this life
and you
can be

that truth that is dripping through?
knocking on your door?

that's the first step to the mystery
unveiling magic where
you never saw it coming

maybe it hurts at first
maybe it's chaos
and wildfires
but the muddy waters will settle

the wind will take you

we can't find freedom

to begin

without the winds of resistance
that take us there

## to begin

feeling our feelings
reconnects us
to our heart
out of the head
into the body
into the heart

you will find
a wisdom there
so beyond your
earthly understanding
sit into *here*
feel the waterfall
of love cascade
inside

## to begin

you don't have to wait
until tomorrow
to open your eyes

you're okay here
it's okay to be scared
to reach out your fingertips
into the unknown
not knowing where
you're headed
but knowing that the trust
that has gotten you
to where you are
will not run out
it will not run up
it lives in your body
and your body is here
to live with you
to live for you

as you look life
in the clear eyes
and say take me
*i am ready*
*i am ready for it all*
and your heart smashes open

## to begin

into a thousand rose petals
all destined
for their reunion
to the whole

to begin

mastery is in the journey
not the destination
and you
my love
are right on time

to begin

once you honor what was
you make space for what is meant to be

to begin

no need to hold on
no need to grasp
no hard holds here

just soft landings
soft touches
soft flows
soft pieces

finding their way
to fit together

## to begin

nostalgic for the life
we are yet to live

nostalgic for the moments
about to happen
that exist
in the fingertips
of this existence

to begin

while all the pieces
might not make sense now
let it not
change
the destination
keep weaving your dream
once stitch at a time
keep reconciling your fears
sit and surrender your worries
to the great light
that gives us life
the sun
send it all up
all the worry
all the fears
shake it off

## to begin

this moment right here
what if it was perfect

the way the blanket wraps around the toes
the way the socks hold it all in place

the way you glance up
and see the heron
gliding perfectly over puget sound

the way the colors outside
invite you inside

the way it all fits like the masterpiece that it is

this moment
with the makings for the life
bigger than your dreams
bigger than your imaginations
bigger than what vision holds for tomorrow


this here moment
right here
holds the answer

                            to begin

for it all

to begin

remain here
in the stillness
calmness
of your heart
where this flower
is slowly
gently
blossoming
and
becoming

to begin

tell me
whisper in my ears
with your soft lips
where in your life can you soften?
the corners of your mouth?
the boundaries of your heart?

to begin




how wild it was










to set it free

## to begin

it's all here. laying dormant inside. waiting. begging. for you to come to know how much of a gift it is to be alive. this world on fire both inside and out. crackling and burning to remind you. to wake you up to the genius of your medicine inside. to slip into spaces where god can dance with you. speak it. say it. let it go. to rewild your story. to rewild your own.

## to begin

stop your running
if it's not working

stop your worry
if it's pulling you down

pick your face up
out of the mud
you don't need to choose to stay face down

return back into the womb of your life
nestle in
get cozy

find your breath
find your moment

what do you see here
what do you allow to land here

no need to be buzzing about
waiting for liquid flight to find you
when it's inside
waiting for you to melt into the space between

no words need spoken

## to begin

just feelings felt
just peace in the space of here

the world will tell you
when it's time to return
back into the epicenter
of you
and your heart
and your beat
your pulse

it's new
it's all so new
fresh
like a perfect daisy in the field
so don't turn your head
don't turn your eyes
return by returning
into the sacred wisdom
of quiet
still
laying
breathing

# to build

to build

drop it all
until all that is left
is you
unrecognizable
to your very own scent

## to build

they tell you to chase
what's electric
and as you do
you witness the addiction
you have to what's burning
red hot
the unquenchable thirst
you have
to a moment
of momentary bliss
where just for one pause
everything is fed
and nourished
and touched
and kissed
the momentary switch
from inhale
to exhale
the pass of peace

to build

if you can sit
and hold *'what is'*
as the most sacred treasure
you can hold it all

to build

open palm
open heart
open life

## to build

i don't want to
grapple anymore of
needing to know
what's next
needing to fill in the blanks
to answer the questions
i want to become friends
with the mystery
the beautiful nature
of not knowing
of sitting into the
stillness of the
*not knowing*
trusting the power of
this river
this conversation with life
i just want to invite in
a deeper grace with
the unknown,
not needing to make
any chess moves
from here,
just feeling the earth
around me
finding love in my breath

## to build

allow the weight to evade you
the illusions to unclip from you
as you take a breath
and arrive
one layer peeled off
of suffocation
of restriction
of trickery

as truth begins to crawl its way
into your vision
your hips
your toes
you heart
fingertips
nose tip
knee caps
elbows
knuckles
mind
and
jaw

softening
softening
softening

             to build

as the resistance
becomes the smoke
of release
from your morning tea kettle
transmuted into new form

## to build

light and dark
love and fear
purpose and pain
sacred and wounding
greatness and smallness
play and destruction
movement and stagnation
all living inside

## to build

get to know your own flow
before you go out there
and try to join another's
your two step
too sacred
to not be seen in the mirror
by the dancer himself
the star of his own show
but never aware of what he looks like
or how his face moves
as he shimmies about the world

to build

people want to know
they want a piece of you
as you weave new pieces of you
islands merging
into more land mass
of love and understanding
hope and miracles
believing and listening
of a life
lived devoted
to the internal compass
delivering its perfect answer
in every moment

## to build

melt like the way the pillow-ey blanket
merges with the sheet below

melt into the slipstream
sipped stream
of even deeper
and deeper
gulps of now

all ears
all paws
all tongues
eyes
graciously opening
to the exhale
of trust
as your whole being
whole body
believes in the placement
and perfection
of it all

so the next breath
can land here
with an even deeper
symphony

## to build

from the space left behind

witness every object around you
turn into wisdom
medicine
a key unlocked
for your holding

letting the matter around
hold the anchor
of hope
and trust
and everything in between
so that the matters of the heart
can
soften
release
allow

as the scenes around
breathe lungs into their own
finally realized
into perfection

to build

believe the heart truth
not the mind story

## to build

does it all just happen in a blink of an eye? and all of these bumps in the road that feels like mountains to climb barefoot are simply there for us to meet ourselves? and see how much we can practice pausing, zooming out, inviting in support, and carrying on? is it to remind us to say i love you more? and hug the ones we keep close, and even the ones we just meet? is it so that we feel the rise of life over our heart and are reminded once again that life is a blessing and a miracle? everyday a new moment to open? a treasure? can we let go enough to remember all of this as we feel time is running out? another story. can we let that fade away like the rest of them? and loosen our grip on time itself and let ourselves land directly into the palm of where we're meant to be? and trust that whatever is meant to be, always will?

to build

the beginning
middle
and end
of each
present current
wave of mystery
answers found
in the questioning
and allowing
completion
full circle
each day arrives
with a new feather of flight
the more you can release
the more will join hands with you
*—love's embrace*

to build

awe and grief
celebration and nostalgia
coming and going
somewhere else and always here

## to build

it's a rotation
a sing song
in and out
yes and no
kind of laugh
each passing your
hand to the
next
with love and ease
and a blessing

the curtain is drawn
and you're still on stage
unaware of the next
move
unaware of the next
still picture

an arrival
fully immersed
into the tendrils
of limitless time
and all the life
that is known
in her invisible
endless hug

## to build

everlasting

with time
and space
for the whole moment
to come online

the little fairy whispers
the dew from the raindrops
the light reflection on the leaf
the space
to so deeply
arrive
into the resonance
of this particular
eternal now

trust the asking
of your eyes
to open
to see
to know
the light
and the warmth
that glows
in

                              to build

what is
already yours

to build

you were too busy
with your wandering eyes
out to the world
worried about making tidal waves
that you forgot
about the power of making ripples
in this current wave of *life*

to build

it is all for you,
do you hear me?
every blade of grass
every strangers eyes you lock
every heart break
every missed bus
every delayed plane
everything is happening for you
please believe this,
and your life will
set sail to places
your imagination
can only taste
*let it all become true*
get the human out
of the way
let it all be
for you –
my love,
*for you*

## to build

we walk around
with baskets
seeking
asking
begging
for them to be filled
by the day
taking
needing
taking some more

giving away
permission
power
medicine

believing the narrative
that it all lives outside of us

forgetting the greatest
non-fiction story of all

sit down
cross legged
let your basket lay in your lap

## to build

close your eyes
find your bounty inside
find the fruits of you
of all that you've tended to
all that is still dripping
it's juicy aliveness for you

find it
find the bounty
find the harvest

fill your basket
with your own wisdom
your own knowing
your own fruits
all different colors
and textures
and tastes and flavors
and medicine
all right here

## to build

time didn't touch us,
we moved slow
and loved hard
and nothing was ever the same

## to build

it's a funny dance, this life. one minute you're feeling the golden hue internally and dancing in your own sunshine. some days, you are so abundant in gratitude and everything you touch turns to gold. and then the dance shifts. and suddenly you can't quite find the rhythm of what used to come as natural to you. you can't quite find your feet and don't know which foot to put forward. you might even forget what your feet look like. maybe you can't even stand. but you play with the dirt. *and the grit.* on the ground. and you learn something about yourself. something that helps you believe you can stand again. something that gives you hope. and you find your footing, *slowly*. and you begin to walk. a little more proud. a little more aware. and you meet other humans who are in this same dance. and you dance together. a new dance. a new you.

and then you stumble. *just a little*. you get back in the grit. back in the dirt. but this time, it's different. because you've been here before. you know you will dance again. you may not fully believe it, but you know you've done it before so you will do it again. you just know. so you allow yourself *to feel*. you allow yourself to play in the dirt. and learn. more about you and what you need and what

## to build

stories you've been living and how your childhood directly affects you. and who you want around you and how you impact people. you collect rain drops.

and this time, it's different. and when you dance again, you bust loose. the sunshine radiates from every cell of your body and skin. and you shine. and make everyone in your path brighter than before. you leave glitter in your glow. you scatter sunshine. you know you'll be back in the grit, you know you'll be back in the raindrops, but you see it now. you need the rain to clear up space for the sun to shine. you see how it's all part of the dance.

some days, you scatter sunshine. other days, you collect rain drops. and that's the dance of life.

to build

life is so much deeper
than the stories we tell

to build

what if there wasn't a moment in a day
when you walked away from yourself?

## to build

all in
yet unattached
present
yet dreaming
here
yet everywhere
grounded
yet soaring
water
yet fire

unaware of the power
that we hold
yet fighting for
the ground to be known

*flow*
she says

*be*
she whispers

find the joy
find the crack of the smile
jump in
clothes on

                                to build

it's a feeling
and it's already here

to build

life has a way
of coming
together
all pieces
in peace

*life has a way*

to build

answers in stillness
patience in love
freedom in structure
courage in truth
adventure in unknown

to build



when we start to share
we start to remember

## to build

slow sips of life
from the taproot
of nourishment
no running here
no sprinting here
no jumping jacks
just simply
the pace of grace

to build

we're meant to *feel*, not run

## to build

how do we know?
how can we tell?
when it's my stuff
or our stuff
or his stuff
or collective stuff?

when do we know
what pieces to
put down
and what pieces
to pick up?

when do we hold our own selves
tenderly?
and when do we let ourselves be held?
as we melt and allow
the tenderness
of grace
soften us into home?

when do we know
that we are leaving for me
and not going for you?

where does the blended line

## to build

of you and me and us come to be?

enmeshment
entanglement
interconnection
woven together

when is it too much to hold?
and when is it okay to put it all down?
to not have to carry the weight anymore
the burden of life crunching our spines

maybe we let them go here
in the space between
the letters of these questions
in the space between
you and me
and what is to be
in the space between
heartbeats
yours and mine
and what we've come to know
as ours

to build

i kill myself
a thousand times over
just to experience life

to build

progress shows up
   and sneaks into the moments
that are most surprising to us
the subtleties
the tiny shifts of feeling
  here and there
 like a light in the fog
   momentary
yet timeless in its essence

## to build

slow down
the pace
of where you're trying
to go

no trying here
just open hearts
and soft minds
relaxed shoulders
and jaw

feet sure of their moment
of movement

it strikes in perfect pace
always
but
like a lightning bolt
to the sky
you must be present
for its hide and seek

always desiring
to know your seek
but knows the power
of the game

## to build

who are you
when it's just you
witnessing you?

no one else
around

no one else
just you

who shows up then?
is she soft?
and kind?

does she move slow
or fast
as she dips from scene to scene?

does she listen to the moment?

or want to fast forward
through it all?

what stories run through you
when it's just you
dancing in the embrace

                              to build

of your own heart
and no one else's?

to build


breathe life
into new found spaces
within this structure
no one ever said flight
could be found on the ground

## to build

barefoot soles
breed
barefoot souls
connected to matter
much greater than
what we touch

let it all go
*the stories*
*the clothes*
*the worries*
*the past*
*the what ifs*
*the layers*
*the weight*

let it all go
so that all that
is left
are your barefoot soles
on the barefoot earth
to breed a barefoot you

as the dross of no longer
flies like the crows
in the wind

to build

one strike
one song
of oneness together
not connected
not anchored
by what we leave behind
but by what is right here

roots crack through
the bottom
the weathered and wise feet
that have stamped you as
timeless
in a timed world

## to build

drift into the world of love
ever present
always here
always ready
to sing its chorus
its anthem
to you
as you return
to an earth
more centered inside
more full of
space and emptiness
a life of light
made possible
by the space between
your toes
as each
lands into their
own sacred unison
of home

to build

let your dreams be your true north

## to build

witness the demise
of that which feeds the belly
to the silver linings

no more silver linings here
we find the golden light
and all she shines her brilliance on
by the whisper of truth
and the ways she reveals her sacred wisdom

listen close enough
to witness the tower falling
collapsing
all we know it to be
dissolving
until all our eyes can see
is the rainbow appearing on the other side

we leap into the space between
that which turns into solid ground
when we keep walking
shakily
sturdily
proudly
confused-ly

## to build

into the spaces yet to have witness our fingerprints
but waiting for our aliveness
to bring it all online

it is here we breathe life
into the truth of our soul
our sacred blueprint

we can't quite fathom how good it will be
but we trust deeply
in the instrument of feeling truth in our body
and we keep hoping
that the whispers of resonance
bring us home
into a symphony of love
greater than the greats once here

to believe

## to believe

what happens when they cross over
no longer in the flesh here
but more alive in spirit
than before

hard to believe
since we have a hard time believing
in the invisible

it's meant to build our trust
build our pact
with something intangible
yet so real

what happens then?
do we release them like a balloon in the wind?
in the sky?
accidentally let loose from the celebration?

or do we sit with their spirit
ask them to whisper to us through the butterflies?
that flicker of light that catches the corner of our eyes?

do we allow ourselves to believe
in something so much more
profound than life happening in the flesh

to believe

and then no longer?

to believe

there is something larger at force here — i know this in my bones

## to believe

what happens when the
sun sets + the rest
softens? and the mind
sees how impermanent
it all is?
and the heart can then
only follow?
do we take responsibility
for the energy we
carry?
and what we allow in?

what do we do to become
friends with time?
+ give up the rest to god?

how do we get messy
when the world says
clean up?

how do we inspire ourselves
to keep living with
our hearts wide
open?

little doorways to conversations

## to believe

of trust + back-flips into
padded floors of beautiful
dreams?

places that feel like home,
when we finally close
our eyes + feel
what we've been looking for
all along?

how do we tie ourselves to
rocketships of trust,
our greatest pump up coach,
the one always cheering us
on, the ones that take
their time?

and live into the sensations
of the seasons?

sometimes, a burning fire
amongst snowy mountains —
other times,
a hot sunny day on the
sparkling water to
watch the golden leaves
drop to their next life,

## to believe

all of us re-lighting
re-igniting
re-alizing
that just by sitting here,
all of this is a miracle
and the only cracks in the
sidewalk we trip over
are the ones we forget
to be really present for —
a trip of the mind,
a moment to return
to the body

look up,
see the light,
see the blue,
feel the hue —
of what it feels
like to really
be alive

look in the mirror + see
the sparkle

that little innocent
being in you,

## to believe

that reflection of truth
+ innocence
+ purity
all locked into your
eyes,

a reminder of how to
return to your heart
when the world wants you
to burn fast —

quick quick,
you might miss it …

move slow

deep breath
here you are,
here you go,
flow

to believe

you are so free
in your rebellion

to believe


people forget it's never personal

to believe

let go of the cocoon
turn into the goo
spread your wings
rise into yourself
one truth at a time

## to believe

we can't forget who we are
we can't look into the mirror
and not remember the story etched
into the wrinkles and freckles
into the sun drenched story
of those endless nights and days
turned weeks where you became one with it all
the sand that tickled you free
the ocean dips that laced you into peace
the lost track of time
and timelines
all melting just as the ocean blue
becomes one with the ocean sky
the perfect mix of elements
to mirror the clearest truth back —
you
you are it all
one cannot exist without the other
so don't forget to love
don't forget to run
into that clear night sky
dipping your whole body
into the sensation of the invitation here
pulling you
*pulllllling* you
ever so gently and patiently

## to believe

like nature does
to let you taste your own
sense of freedom here
to let your tongue hang out
to remember this moment
this moment you chose
this miracle around
that is you

to believe


birds find flight
regardless
of the weather

to believe










winning is in
the feeling of it

## to believe

hope catches you
in moments when you forget

when you've turned off
the switches around you
yet
somehow
around the corner
comes the whisper
bearing her belly
her flesh
for you to remember
your own

becoming the full
belly breasted
reminder
of how to keep
our love alive

to believe

falling
*upright*

## to believe

they say miracles only happen in fairytales and tall tales. but i see rainbows. and birds flying right through the sky in the perfect moment. i see clouds putting on a show to bring all of the colors alive. i see it. as i pause on the side of the road to look up. i see the way the clouds meet the light which holds the rainbow. i see the bird fly right over. i see it all. big moments are these small moments, really. where miracles come alive just by simply witnessing. taking a breath. coming home again to the wild nature of this life. none of us truly in the knowledge of how we got here. or how we have brains and hearts. and toes and fingertips. how we have the gift of crying to allow rivers to come through our eyes. and laughing to allow our body to bellow with aliveness. i think this is the fairytale. it's a real tale. it's here. the big reveal. heaven on earth has always been. and we are finally opening our eyes to the mere miracle begging to be witnessed by the present eye.

to believe

tell me truth
and nothing else

to believe

the crackle of the fire
let that be enough

the way the sip of water
refreshes your whole system
let that be enough

dropping deeper and deeper
not into the whisper
of what you know
but into the whisper
that calls out
your thirst for curiosity

and begs you to be
no nowhere
but here

to believe






you are electric when you follow your intuition

## to believe

god finds us in moments
of tangible presence

sipping morning coffee
making pancakes
walking in stride
with flowers
by our side

continuing to create space
to source ourselves
from the eternal
internal
yet external
galaxy of it all
being
right
here

constantly allowing
the pull
to take these bodies
into their version
of flight

as the pushing

to believe

starts to release its grip

to believe

patience is sweet in moments
yet fierce in its essence
it has claws
and teeth
and grit
for something beyond
it knows the truth
and begs
to be honored
in its quest
of an honest
revolution

to believe

people want a piece
of those who are flying
forgetting the flight
that lives inside

to believe

may the gates
of today
open with beauty
and all of us
present for its whispers

to believe

it only ever was the small things

to believe

it had to be unbelievable
in order
for us to start believing

to believe

we are dreams still dreaming

to believe

no longer chasing
what is innately us

to believe

the work you're doing with your heart
touches deeper than you know

## to believe

what if you were meant to fly
to soar
to rise higher than the sky
right in the moments
when you feel your whole ground crumbling
right when you feel that you're destined for the end

the bottom
the crash

what if this was your beginning

the moment

when you looked in the mirror
and saw the hero of your own eyes
the wisdom of your own freckles
the shimmering of truth around your skin
the depth of all that you've breathed
and all that you've survived

what if this was the moment
it all
ignited for you

the moment you decided to stay

## to believe

to stay with yourself
your tender heart
your aching bones
your stretched throat

devoted to giving voice
to the voiceless parts of you

devoted to seeing this mystery through
so that the mission of your soul
can be known simply by witnessing you

what if today
you realized
that the hardest parts of life
are already over
that you've won
and now it's just the practice of it all

of choosing tears over swallowed truths
sacred rage over repressed fire
spoken truths over bit tongues

continuing to dance
and fall in love
with every
bleeding

## to believe

blooming
burning
banishing
breaking
and
building
part inside of you

with every
rising
pulsing
igniting
sensation
and season
of how you came to be
and how you continue to be
pulsing
rising
igniting
through it all

what if this was the moment
you became the phoenix
who rose from the dust
of her own ashes

every crumbled part

## to believe

reborn
regenerated
as gasoline
and fuel
for the new life
of you
and all she spreads her wings for

soar
like the wild one that you are
bound to none
caged by nothing
and open to it all

to believe

there is an entire universe inside of you begging for
permission to express itself

## to believe

made it to the top of the mountain
let the belly
lay flesh
along the long
wooden tree

it is here
where presence is found
where this breath
finds language in the space between
in and out
where this heart
finds language in the space between
expand and contract

it is here
where all comes to be

the wandering stories of the past
the present musings of the now
the string of excitements
and unknowns of the tomorrows

it is here
where this being
feels still enough

to believe

to be felt
safe enough
to melt

for it is here
where these eyes lay
on the soft cheeks
of the trees growing
with the mountains

the marriage of
earth and wind
sun and rain
human and nature

to believe

when we are ready
the invitation appears

to believe

keep walking
because you are
worth the feeling
of being on
the other side

## to believe

it's times like these
in places like this
where we remember
as remembering slips into
the holes of forgetting

not long ago
were these drapes
filled with empty spaces
confused at the direction
and purpose
of this fall

but sit in
cozy up
she will reveal to you
her greatest show
wisdom overflowing
honey dripping
until the grand reveal
is felt
like sunlight
beaming warmth
over you all

remember the way the light

to believe

hit the morning dew
on that single blade of grass


remember the last blink of light
as you watch him dip behind the horizon

remember the breath
when you remembered to breathe

all the tiny mementos
we collect
that add color to it all

## to believe

allow yourself to be immersed
nothing a mistake
no wrong turns
just light reflecting light
darkness holding the duality
your eyes
allowing a small part
of the disco ball
make sense to us all

these
these are the rivers
of remembrance

when we are quiet enough
still enough
brave enough
to touch it
feel it
hear it
see it
and experience it all

## to believe

i wonder what it is that
the sun says to the
world when it starts
to dip above the horizon
wake everyone up
let them know that
another day has arrived

i wonder what it's like
to be a force that huge
with radiance that powerful

and then i remember
that we are –
forces
of nature
when we nurture
our hearts
when we expand
with our minds
when we free ourselves
from the ties holding us
back
from the weight

to believe

carried on our shoulders

to believe

may the depths
of your truth
set you free

to believe

love is what it comes back to
and to love
is to be brave
to love
is to speak the textures
of truths from the deepest
vulnerable parts of you and me
like the way the moss
whispers to the tree
forever dancing
entangled
in a love story greater
than the movies

to believe

barefoot toes
barefoot heart
not knowing
what tomorrow brings
but knowing
what we will bring tomorrow
our whole hearts
our two feet
open palm
open fist
open mouth
chin tilted back
tasting the rain

## to believe

you're going to blink
and ten years of life are going to pass
just like the last ten did
and they're going to look the same —

unless you're showing up every day
with a little more willingness
to listen a little bit deeper
to open a little softer
to show up with a little more presence
and to act with a little more courage

as you ruthlessly
unravel
the gravity of them
and relentlessly
devote yourself
to the gravity of you
and what your body craves
and what your heart beats for

one day you're going to wake up
and realize that it was all one big
playground
and the moments that seemed so big
we're micro moments

## to believe

in the grand scheme of things

you're going to wake up to the fact
that your truth is the most potent medicine
and everyone might not understand
but your heart doesn't understand
when you choose the stiffness
of the mind games
instead of the softness
of the heart ground

one day you're going to wake up
to the fact that you're becoming
the big kid
that your little kid inside needed
when the world felt loud
and scary
and unsafe
when all she or he wanted to do
was belong and love and be loved
but was programmed
to believe otherwise

but it's all making sense now
it's all connecting now

you're going to wake up

## to believe

and ten years of life are going to pass —
and it's going to look the same and feel the same
unless you look in the mirror one day
with your feet so gently rooted into the earth
and say —

this is my *one* life
in this body
this is my *one* life
to live this life
to lean into the wildness of my nature
the ridiculousness of my magic
the depth of my wisdom
and the trust of my heart
and so bravely
and tenderly
decide
no longer for the gravity of them —
reclaiming the gravity of you

to belong

# to belong

## to belong

i trace my etchings of this moment
down tree lined roads

nowhere to go
but into the gray haze in front of me

just enough
to see the next clue
to feel safe enough
to deliver myself into the next reveal
safe enough
to keep my foot on the gas
to feel the stirrings
of what comes alive in my heart
when i allow it all
to pulse into me

no more surges plugged in out there
only flight from in here
and all the different truths
that quiver their moment for me

i trace the etchings of this moment
down tree lined roads
with nothing but the true next move revealed

## to belong

i watch the birds fly above
in perfect union
with grace
and joy
and purpose

i see the way the owl landed
on that sign
to give me a sign
of the wisdom dripping from within

all of this outside world
in place
because of this inside world

open up to your own tree lined road inside
where the birds whisper their freedom to you
where the bunnies bring in their luck for you
where the hummingbirds buzz in delight for you
where the corners of this whole earth meet

earthquakes and wildfires
waterfalls and hurricanes
truth and nothing else

## to belong

what you appreciate
appreciates you

what you love
loves you

what you're present for
is present for you

it really is
the simplest equation

maybe all of life works
like this

the simplest
purest
straight to the point

bullseye
answers

go slow
listen loud
love more

## to belong

speak more truths
speak more fears
look up
find all of your senses here
breathe deep
appreciate every single thing
go when your heart calls
stay when she doesn't

find the perfect stranger
of every moment
every scene
opening you
more and more
to love

more and more
to how good it can be
how open your heart can truly be
how clearly your stride will
always take you

into the perfect moment
at the perfect time

every bite
every glance

## to belong

every heard bird
every lived moment
fully alive
by your awareness of it

## to belong

we arrived just in time
to have a say in our lives

## to belong

wear the same clothes for 5 days
shower in the lake and the sea
learn every trace of your own scent
without the stuff and stories of them

camp at the site of your own heart
wake up to the morning light
that peaks within
lay on the footprint of your own soul
let go of any light outside of yourself

see what comes alive
in your grit
in the dirt beneath your fingernails
in the oil of your hair
in the way your skin feels
after dipped in water and wind

let go of the stories that hold you hostage
to the character you aren't anymore

your character is brazen
and built from the wildfires
that burn inside

let the musings of your

## to belong

slumbering genius awaken
let your heartstrings pluck open
let curiosity lead the way
follow that call
follow that voice inside
wake up that genius inside
we are ready to hear you roar

## to belong

it's heartbreaking, really. to sit in the window of the train as the world speeds by. and realize the impermanence of it all. of every moment. every bite. every smile. every trip. every adventure. every sip of water. every moment coded with its own specific whisper of meaning. all placed for the listening. it's heartbreaking, really. when you realize how simple it all is. how easy it can all be when we stop trying to figure it out. how the dots connect. how the heart makes sense again. how it all is more beautiful than what we dreamt up. as we live the moments we've only lived up in our minds. and weeks or months later, you are witnessing it all come to fruition. zoom out for a moment, to realize the omen of it all. it's heartbreakingly beautiful, really. the weaving that we allow. the goodbyes that rename themselves as hellos. each moment a gateway to the divine. each moment a portal into something richer than what our fingertips could describe to our lips. the world spins by. and we move with it.

## to belong

*that* cord. *that* sensation. *that* feeling. *that* lightning. *that* is the one. that is what you crave. that is what you beg of. that is the energy that requests you. sit at the altar of peace and know your name. stand at the base of the mighty oak and remember where you came from. catch the subtle light, and come home to your darkness. not the kind where you sit in aloneness, stuck in stories of separation, but into the density that makes the levity known. the opposites. like polar bears scratching on tree. don't stay long in places that confuse you. don't stop for strangers that cause you to dizzy the dust of your magic. choose your aliveness. go after that. while everyone is out there counting their dollars, count the amount of times each day you felt alive. and added logs to your fire. and tended to the beautiful things. the tiny tinders. the flicker of life that you are comes and goes. don't let life come and go without knowing its name, and you really knowing yours.

to belong

i attune myself
to the frequency
of freedom now

*and repeat*
*and repeat*
*and repeat*

to belong

unspoken truths lay
like that tight
bedsheet from those
five star hotels

tucked and prodded
perfectly

so tight
so constricting
so debilitating to life
your life force
the energetic movement
in your body

slowly let the bed sheet release
as you unclench your jaw
and open to the world
that comes alive
when you speak
what's true for you

## to belong

i think sometimes we forget that we are meant to experience true magic while we are here. miracles. the life of our greatest dreams *and then some*. that we are meant to realize the power of all that we have the ability to create. i think sometimes we think that maybe we're just meant to keep circling and keep circling, without ever allowing ourselves to experience the divine richness that comes from letting our prayers come into reality. of the dream version of you and the dream partner and the dream home and the dream travel destinations. and the dream ways of being and engaging with others. all of it. all of them. you're meant to experience them. you're meant to get in that car and go. and book that flight. and talk to strangers and spend days on end just reading random books by the fire. that it all gets to come to you when you return to yourself. and it's not a path of glory. it's a path of all of the things you already know to do. and discipline or devotion or commitment are the gas in the tank that get you believing in yourself. that you can. and you will. *and you are.*

to belong

hold each other
on the petals
of each other's
most sacred flowers
on the flutter
of each other's wings

## to belong

it's all the *'in between everything'* moments where my feet find the water, and my body melts. it melts so purely i can't help but see the magic that is transpiring right in front of my eyes. this life, alchemy. these roads we live, pure. how could we ever allow ourselves to be contained in a box? breathe bigger breaths into the moments that can so easily escape us. let us feel the embrace of leaning back and carrying on from here. let us let the love into the crevices of our hearts we hold for ourselves. for this life is ours for the making, and i'm making it sparkle at its own reflection. here's to this life we get to live, and the full body extension of living alive while we are here.

## to belong

you are the magic
and you are the mountain
you are the rain
and you are the sahara
you are the roots of the trees
and the nectar of the bees
mercy
mercy
mercy

## to belong

perhaps that is what so much of life is about

seeing the constructs of self we build up
based on the constructs of life around us
and what it tells us
and how we hear it

perhaps that's what happens
as time moves us forward
we hear differently
vibrations land differently
placed differently
in the ear drum
heart drum
hum
of that which we call our life

releasing what we once held
as truth knocks
and reveals a new version
of how the story wants to be told
of how you want to be told

we bathe in what is no longer
as we watch our hands try to
grasp

## to belong

grieve
onto what still is
yet no longer
carries oxygen
for what's here

perhaps this is how the story wants to go
in its own time
in its own hymn and hum
of self
divine self
highest self

not the self we hold and see from here
but from the self that knows
how precious this moment is
how precious this version of us is
and the version of those we meet around the table

perhaps this is the biggest blessing of all
a miracle really
that this moment
this self
this vision
will never be again
never quite like this
no two feelings the same

## to belong

constantly moving like the tides
and the clouds that morph and reorganize

never restricting the flow

so we play with what arrives
old stories finding new meanings
old ways practicing into fresh flesh

realizing the only scene we've changed
is that what feeds the mind's eye

the beliefs we hold
the thoughts that feed them
and the meaning we give them

perhaps we are meant to meet ourselves here
allowing the stories to dismantle
the visions to be left to breath
and the heartbeat
to be king of all

## to belong

we are butterflies
forever dancing
in the oneness of delight

## to belong

life lived
in the present droplets of now
the breeze of hot summer air
on the landscape of this skin
earth soaked —
with the cathedral
of it all

simple musings
want life to be enough
exactly as it is

every single piece
in its divine order
as long as it is listening
knowing when to burn up
when to cool down
when to simmer
when to speak
when to glisten
when to share
when to simply intimately
exist in the moment

no pictures needed
no stories needed

## to belong

just come
feel the pulse of this heart
feel this skin,
and you will know

just come
i don't want to speak words
i want to be felt
and known
in the intangibility
of my pulse
coming alive
from days spent
soaked in nature
reminded
guided
shown
brought back
to the center
bloodline
of it all

## to belong

the waves come
like the rainstorm outside

every hour

it drenches us
and then clears
and clears
and comes again

why do we resist
why do we try to figure out
what we're feeling and why
why do we cling to that which feels safe
cozy
familiar

is there anything wrong with it
is there anything not right about it

we decide
when the clock strikes 12
and let the minute hand
do its thing

this part
let her speak her wisdom

to belong

let her rain
sprinkle you
drench you
with deeper layers
of this potent wisdom

## to belong

clarity is your birthright
love is your home
freedom is the language you are fluent in
never forget how found you already are

## to belong

you aren't one person. with one dream. you are *many* parts. with *many* needs. and *many* dreams. you are both somewhere back there. and right here. and over there. you are bigger than what the house can hold. you are stronger than what you think. you are wiser than the stories from the gurus you read. you are made up of star dust. god particles. universal magic. so while you are here, dream bigger that the walls. dream louder than the voice of fear. rip off all of the lids on the pots that you so carefully touch. live without a roof on your dreams. get wild with it. get dirty with it. get gritty with it. stop fighting for your limitations. stop looking with eyes of scarcity. let your eyes twinkle for that life that feels so absolutely ridiculous *'there is no way'* it could be. there is *'there is no way'* that all that you desire *and then some* could be. be a stand for *those* possibilities. water those seeds in your mind. give breath to those lifelines. land into *that* life while you're here.

to belong

you can't expect a miracle without
seeing the miracle that you already are

## to belong

like a quick dip
in the purest of waters
not needing to stay long
just long enough to remember
the fire that is ignited
and it's forward momentum from here

## to belong

love me. love me even when i don't want to be loved. or touched. or tangled up with. love me. love me on days when i can't bear to see my own reflection. when all i see turns me into a simmer of low heat. and all that once moved feels stuck. love me. love me in moments where my breath seems to bring ice. where belief no longer has a pulse. when the story of hope loses the microphone of now. love me. love me when i can't see beyond the blinding ice storm of fear. and all in the body moves into contraction. love me. love me even when i choose something that stretches you. following the blinks of truth. unraveling it all and finding it all at once. love me on the days when anything i touch turns to gold. and love me on the days when the rainstorms won't leave my side. love me on the days when all i want is a cuddle. a squeeze. your touch. your warmth. and love me on the days when my belly laughter doesn't leave space for words. just joy. without a lid. love me wild. in all of my colors. my rawness. my power. my wildfire inside. my soft gentle breeze. love me surely. and loudly. and proudly. love me through it all.

to belong

two feet in
or none at all

## to belong

sometimes the biggest mirrors are
the quiet spaces
with a pulse bigger than our own
*heart beats*
that simply hold us
in all we have ever been
all we have ever released
and all we will become

## to belong

it's just so wild, this life. everything is temporary. yet those temporary things leave permanent marks on our heart. as much as we try non-attachment, things attach to our hearts. and stay with us. but in each moment we're morphing and changing and evolving. in each moment we're expanding, connecting, contracting, disconnecting. like life is just but a thousand little moments of humanness mixed into our souls and hearts. it's just really a big adventure of love. matters of the heart. open. close. share. shut down. learn. share. share. share. this is the way through and the reason why we're here. hug each other. love each other. we're in this dance together – let's lean more into the universal. more into the likeness and similarities. we've all had dark sad days, moments, months. we've all been lost and confused and filled with fear. can't we hug and love each other through? and laugh at the humanness of it all?

## to belong

i wonder where your mind escapes to
when you move from place to place
when it's just you
and the world
and your mind
and your heart

i wonder where your mind trickles to
what thoughts come alive
in the space between

i wonder what stories play out as you close your
eyes at night
and it's just you
and the ending of your day
and the beginning of your dreams

do you plant seeds
do you replay the day
do you harvest your bounty
do you skip to tomorrow
like a rock across a lake

do you feel powerful
as you drip across into the next phase of your life
do you look back on your day

## to belong

and see it with light and love
or does your mind wander
into things that aren't yours to touch

i wonder if you stay present in your day
or if you think about your tomorrows or yesterdays

i wonder
as i wander
about what
i'm wondering about too

i wonder if you see your life as a canvas
each bite a brushstroke
each spoken truth a glimmer of hope in the night
sky
each nanosecond of courage
an unraveling of the next creative piece

i wonder if you see each day
as the potentiality of a big reveal
for something larger than you could ever fathom
in that sweet mind of yours

i wonder if you feel and know the difference
of your heart and your mind
and what's teaching you these days

## to belong

i wonder how you're listening
and how far you let yourself wander
how many new edges you meet each day
how many parts of you come alive

i wonder
as i wander
into the makings of it all

## to belong

let curiosity
be the crumbling
let inquiry
hold the key
let the walls
dissolve
fall away
until all that is standing
is you and me
and the pulse
of our hands
pounding for a
truth too simple
for us to comprehend —
we are visiting
we are visiting
we are visiting

## to belong

that's the thing about you and me
and our neighbors that we pass on the streets
we're just one huge beating heart

to belong

put your hands up to the sky
feel the structure of your being
perfectly built for love
and the life you've been asking for
as the masks drop
and begin to reveal themselves
in their perfect timing

## to belong

the stars reminded me
that there is space
for us all
to be as we are
and all have our moment

that there is power in stillness
and showing up every day
regardless of clear or cloudy skies

that sometimes we fall
and turn into someone's wish
earth side

that we all dance together
and commune
and light up the sky
in our own beautiful ways

## to belong

what matters when it's all said and done? what truly matters? that we chose love when we could have chosen fear? that we picked up the pieces of trash when no one was looking? that we held the door for our neighbor even if it added a few minutes to our commute? that we spoke every lick of truth from our hearts? even when we were scared? scared to run into the unknown? even though we knew it to be the field of possibility?

what matters most? that we held every single human around us in the energy of compassion? that we transcended our separateness? that we listened to the guidance of our own intuitions? and needed no other evidence or explanation to follow it? that we said the hard thing? that we were present for those around us? that we trusted energy more than words? that we trusted in something greater than ourselves? and saw the screenplay of our lives as scenes happening *for* us? that we lived in integrity with our hearts above all? and ate chocolate for lunch if that's what our body craved?

what matters most? that we showed up for the little things? the sweet moments where the two of you drop everything and embrace? that you feel the

## to belong

connection of all between the connection of you two? that we listened to the shifting of seasons? and placed our hands on the ground and felt the pulse of something greater? and allowed ourselves to feel it all? that we asked mama ocean to speak to us? and saw every moment as the medicine that we needed? that we chose to speak our desires and yet didn't get attached? that we loved big? in all of the ways?

i trust in now. in this moment. in you and me. i trust in our wings and the questions that give us flight.

to belong

aren't you proud?
of the life that has birthed
from the quakes of your own heart?

## to belong

go your own way —
your own book of knowledge
your own heart textures
for the life that wants to be watered from your
bones

love and let go
of the limiting stories
of the parts still holding on
and embrace the source
of power and light within

ask for what's ready to be loved
to be loved
hug these parts
*these inner children*
and set them free to go be —
to go paint the sidewalk
to go bake random made up recipes
to go play hide and seek
to go climb up the trees
*barefoot and free*

because barefoot and free
was all you were ever destined to be

## to belong

it's moments like these
when we are brought to my knees
from the immense amount of beauty around us
and the only words that spill out
are
*thank you*
*thank you*
*thank you*
for it all

## to belong

it is joy
it is joy
it is joy
and it is love
like you've never experienced before

can you contain it?
just for one breath longer?
let it be medicine for the cracks
and crevices
that are forgotten
when we so quickly
disperse it out?

can you close
your eyes
for one moment longer
and really feel this feeling?
for you
and no one else?

let it sink all the way into your cells
a remembering
planted
only by
truly feeling

## to belong

a remembering
planted only
by truly feeling

feel it all the way in
ignite it all the way down to your toes
feel it
drink it
bury it deep
into the forest of your belly
the ocean of your toes
into the sky of your heart
the wind of your existence

and when you're ready
to come
up for air
to share

do it with every ounce of you
do it with every corner of presence
do it with every lick of gratitude
this is love
and you are worthy of it all

to belong

find treasure
in each moment,
warmth in each
word, presence
in each breath

## to belong

the feeling of heart talk
*soft speak*
reflecting the goodness back
to each other,
it's like a thread is in the air
and you can't help but
feel the soft pulse
it brings you into
people are just so beautiful
i think i'm in love with them all

## to belong

"who am i?"
she whispers
she murmurs —

*here*
*come take my hand*
*let us bring*
*our toes*
*to the edge*
*of the river —*
*let me show you*
*who you are*

we arrive

*you see?*
*you are flow and fantasy*
*you are rough and smooth*
*all at once*
*you are the sun*
*that hits water*
*you are*
*the glimmer*
*of light*
*she holds*
*in her reflection*
*you are vast*

## to belong

*you are deep*
*you are wise*
*you are true*

*you are the heartbeat*
*the harmony*
*of it*
*all*
*arriving*
*here*

*you are the strength*
*and integrity of the basin*
*that holds it*

*you are limitless*
*you are infinite*
*you are Home.*

## to belong

and to you reader, i give you the pen. and the blank page to write your book from here. what story wants to unearth itself from your sturdy bones? what life wants to be painted from the tips of your fingers? and the breadth of your span of imagination? go out there and make it magic. make it beautiful. make it wonderful. hug the ones you love close. **find your sure song** every day. notice how the texture changes. notice how your beat always remains. trust the goodness of life. and enjoy the ride. *oh please*, enjoy the ride.

to belong

anna cassedy o'neill writes regularly about the magic of life in her online substack. she also runs an online writing community where the group explores the depths in which words can take us and how connected we all are.

*follow along her writing journey and join the party:*

www.thisonemagiclife.substack.com for weekly musings of This One Magic Life


allaboutbiglove.mn.co to join her online writing community Big Love

to belong

*stay light*
*bless your golden way*

www.ingramcontent.com/pod-product-compliance
Lightning Source LLC
LaVergne TN
LVHW021804060526
838201LV00058B/3233